Elias Hill
101 So Bad, They're Good Doctor Jokes
Copyright 2017
Self-published, Tiny Camel Books

Tiny Camel Books
tinycamelbooks.com
tinycamelbooks@gmail.com

# 101

## So Bad, They're Good

# Doctor Jokes

## By: Elias Hill

**Illustrations By: Katherine Hogan**

If you have a bad cough, take a bunch of laxatives.

That should scare the cough right out of you.

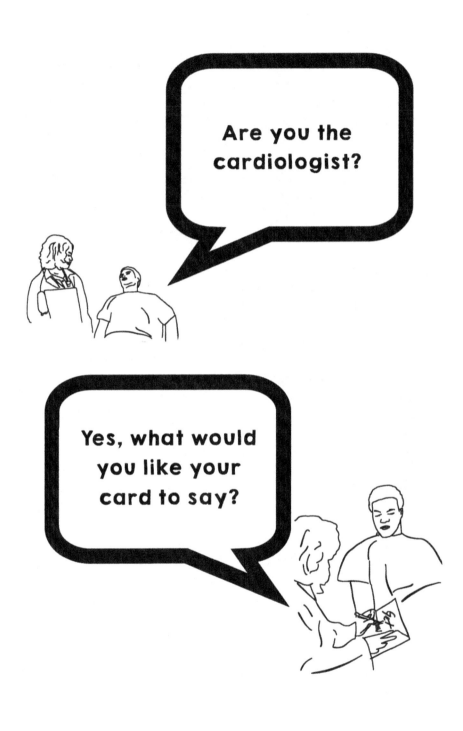

My other doctor said I needed to drink more and exercise less.

Is that so, Mrs. Banks?

Yes, and please, call me My Other Doctor.

Ms. Thomas what's there to be afraid of? The exam? The shots?

The scale.

How's the patient in Room 310?

Probably not going to make it.

Good, I could use a new liver.

Doctor, Monday I had eight silent gas emmisions. Yesterday it was six and today it's already been four. What should I do?

Probably take a hearing test.

You're in luck! We have two hearts available for transplant. One was a teacher's and the other a lawyer's.

I'll take the lawyer's.

He probably never used his.

Doctor, I think I'm suffering from memory loss.

Alright, would you mind paying in advance then?

All day long my son lies in bed and eats yeast and car wax. What will happen to him?

Don't worry, eventually he will rise and shine.

The best doctor is actually a veterinarian.

She can't ask her patient what the problem is.

The worst time to have a heart attack?

Probably during a game of charades.

Doctor, my hair keeps falling out. Have you got anything to keep it in?

What about a shoebox?

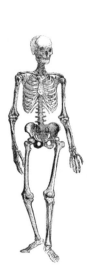

I'm here for my checkup.

I wish you'd come to me sooner.

Doctor, it really hurts when I touch my neck.

Well, don't touch it.

That'll be $75.

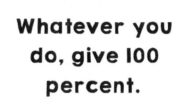

An radiologist and a surgeon are both running to catch an elevator. How can you tell the two apart?

The radiologist sticks his hand in to stop the elevator, the surgeon puts his head in.

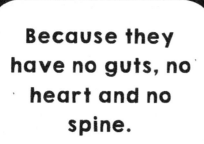

In med school I couldn't decide between proctology and neurology.

So it was heads or tails.

I saw a patient last month who was terribly injured when he fell into an upholstery machine.

Fortunately, he's fully recovered.

How do you hide money from a primary care physician?

Trick question. There's no money in primary care.

Doctor, I get so nervous and frightened during driving tests.

Don't worry about it. You'll pass eventually.

Pass? I'm the examiner!

Why do EMTs travel in sets of two?

They want to be PAIR-a-medics.

Here's a list of our heart, liver and lungs donors in alphabetical order.

Wow, very organ-ized.

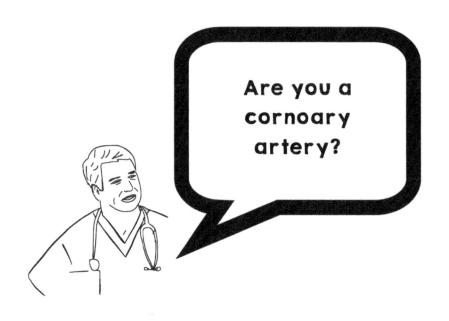

So you don't smoke or drink? You don't do anything that races your heart?

Nope. I don't eat any bad food. I'm 75 and hoping to live another five years.

What for?

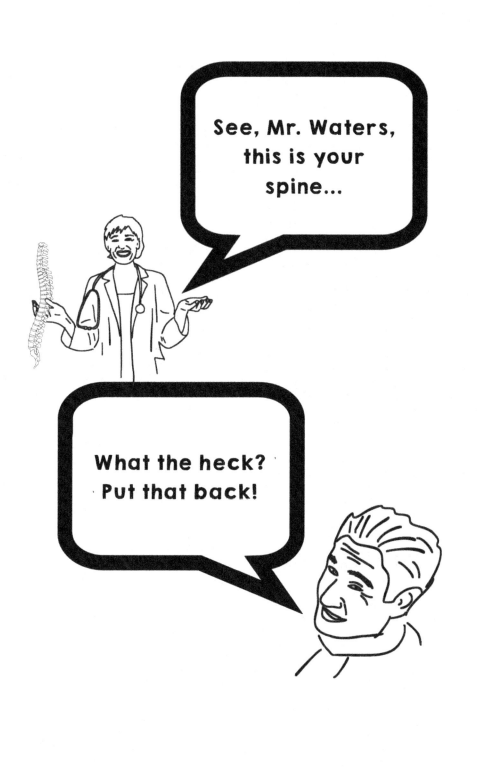

The quickest way to a man's heart?

A bilateral incision on the upper left region of the sternum.

You know that feeling you get when you meet someone and your heart skips a beat?

That's called arrhythmia and you can die from that.

Doctor, I broke my arm in three places.

Stop going to those places.

Does an apple a day keep the doctor away?

Yes, but only if your aim is good.

I have some bad news and some very bad news. The lab called with your test results. They said you have twenty-four hours to live.

Twenty-four hours! Thats terrible! What could be worse? What's the very bad news?

I've been trying to reach you since yesterday.

I'm afraid I have some bad news. You're dying and you don't have much time. You pretty much have ten...

Ten? Ten what? Months? Weeks? What?!

10...9...8...7...

I've got very bad news - you have a bladder infection and Alzheimer's.

Well at least I don't have a bladder infection.

Doctor, I hurt all over. I touch my cheek, it hurts. I touch my ear, it hurts. I touch my foot, it hurts.

You have a broken finger.

Doctor, are you sure I'm suffering from a fever? I heard once about a doctor treating someone with a fever and then she died of typhus.

Don't worry, it won't happen to me. If I treat someone with a fever she will die of a fever.

A boy in my class asked me to play doctor.

Oh dear, what happened?

Nothing, he made me wait 45 minutes and then double-billed the insurance company.

I keep seeing spots in front of my eyes.

Have you ever seen a doctor?

No, just spots.

Are you an organ donor?

No, but I once gave an old piano to Goodwill.

How many doctors does it take to change a light bulb?

That depends on whether it has health insurance.

Your hearing is perfect. Your family must be really pleased that you can hear again with your new hearing aid.

Oh, I haven't told my family yet. I just sit around and listen to their conversations. I've changed my will three times!

If you can't afford a doctor go to the airport.

You get a free x-ray, a tissue exam and saying a few key phrases can get you a colonoscopy.

Doctor, I swallowed a twenty dollar bill.

Let's see if there's any change.

Hey, doc, as a mechanic I basically fix broken parts and make things run like new. So why don't I get paid the big bucks like you?

Try doing it with the engine running sometime.

It's been one month since my last visit and I still feel miserable.

Did you follow the instructions on the medicine I gave you?

I sure did - the bottle said 'keep tightly closed.'

As you can see, this patient limps because his right fibula and tibia are radically arched.

Now what would you do in a case like this?

I suppose I would limp too.

Congratulations!
It's a girl!

I think I'll name
her Eva.

I'm sorry that name is
taken. You can choose
Eva544, Eva_G22,
EvaSoup62...

What's the condition of the cowboy who slipped on the horse manure?

Stable.

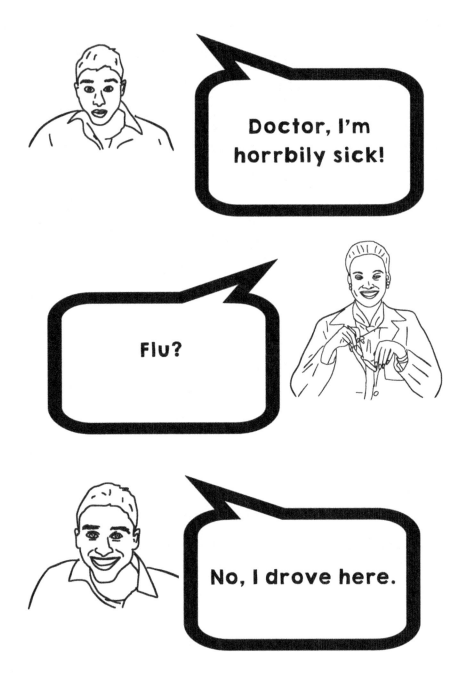

You have acute appendicitis.

Compared to whom?

I exercise all the time.

Really?

Yes, I jump to conclusions, climb the walls, drag my heels, push my luck, make mountains out of molehills, bend over backward, run around in circles, put my foot in my mouth, beat around the bush...

On a scale of zero to ten, what would you say your pain level is?

Oh, I don't know. I'm not good with math.

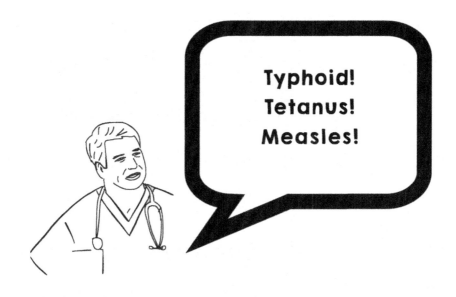

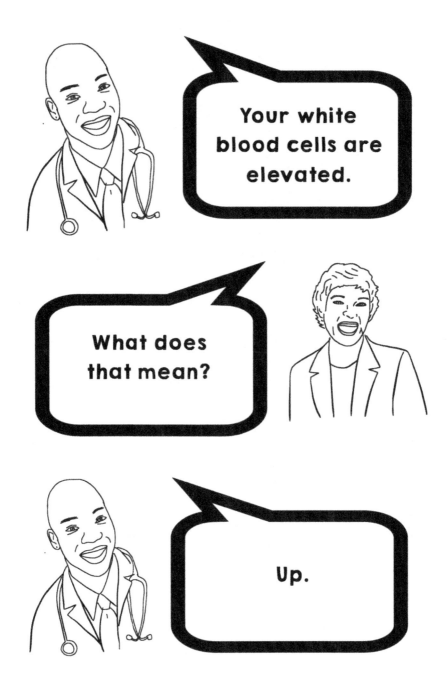

Which do you want first, the good news or the bad news?

Give me the good news.

You're about to have a disease named after you.

Doctor! My wife's in labor and she keeps screaming, 'Shouldn't, couldn't, wouldn't, can't..."

Oh, that's okay, she's just having contractions.

I'll be about 15 minutes late. That won't be a problem, will it?

No, we just won't have time to give you an anesthetic.

I'm sorry to bother you so late, but I think my wife has appendicitis.

I removed that two years ago. Whoever heard of a second appendix?

You may not have heard of a second appendix, but surely you've heard of a second wife.

I heard the nurse say, It's a very simple operation. Don't worry, I'm sure it will be all right.

She was just trying to comfort you. What's so frightening about that?

She wasn't talking to me. She was talking to the doctor!

CPSIA information can be obtained
at www.ICGtesting.com
Printed in the USA
LVOW13s0248221217
560532LV00026B/994/P